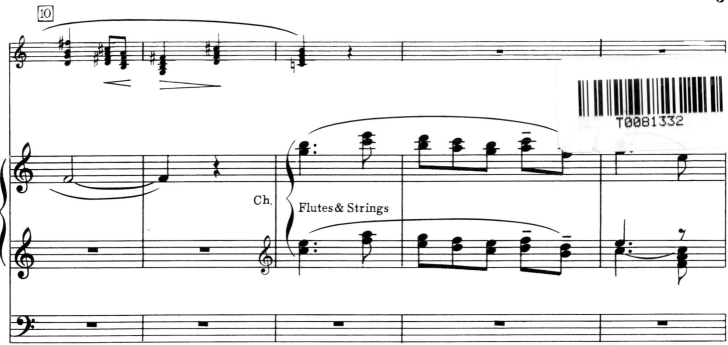

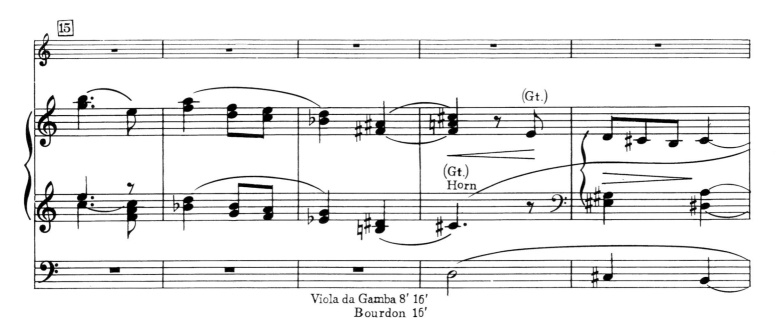

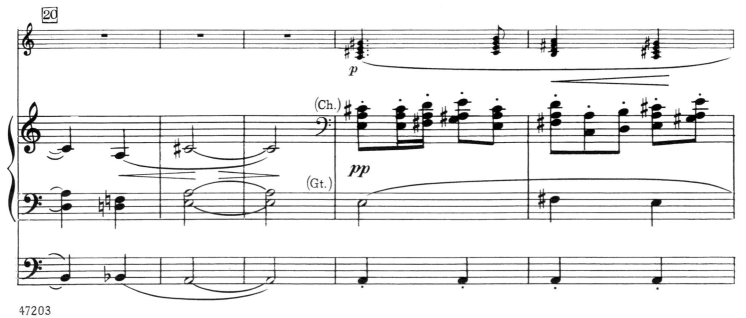

47203

4

Paul Creston

Meditation

for Marimba and Organ

G. SCHIRMER, Inc.

DISTRIBUTED BY

MEDITATION
For Marimba and Organ

Second movement of Concertino
For Marimba and Orchestra, Op. 21
Arranged by the Composer

PAUL CRESTON

47203c

MEDITATION

Marimba

PAUL CRESTON

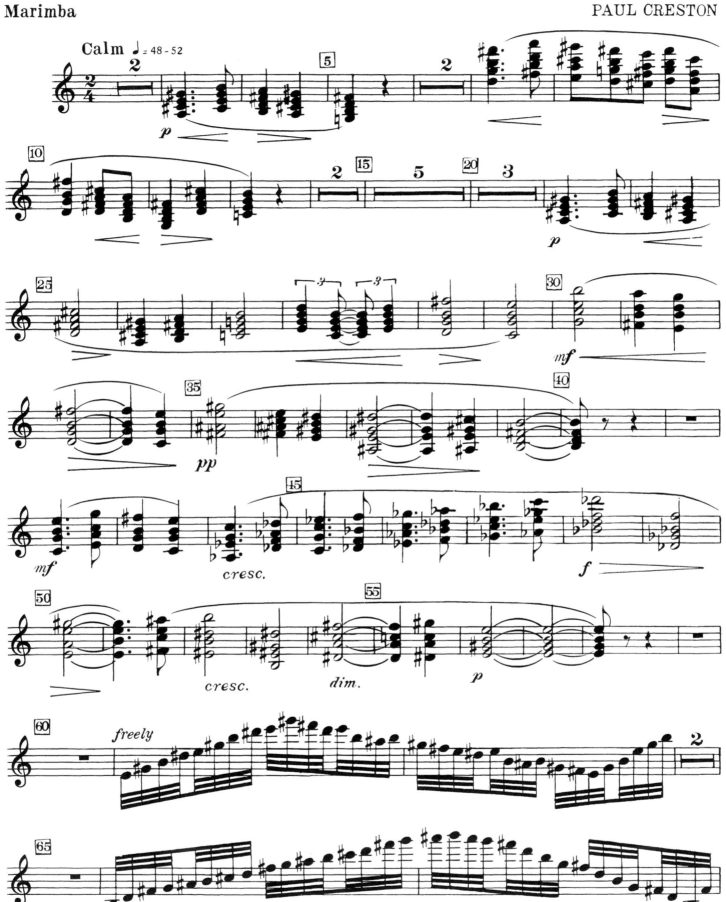

47203c

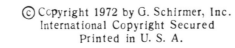

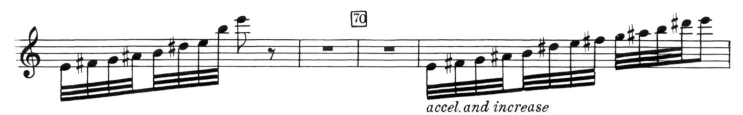

accel. and increase

In time ♩=72

mf ——————— sf

Tempo I

p

increase

f

In time

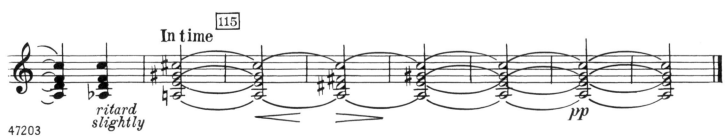

ritard
slightly

pp

47203

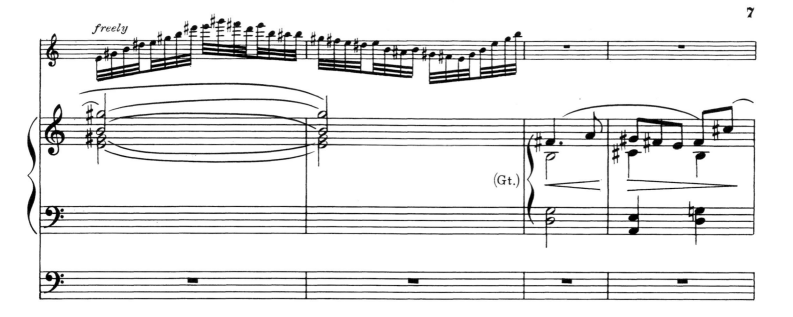

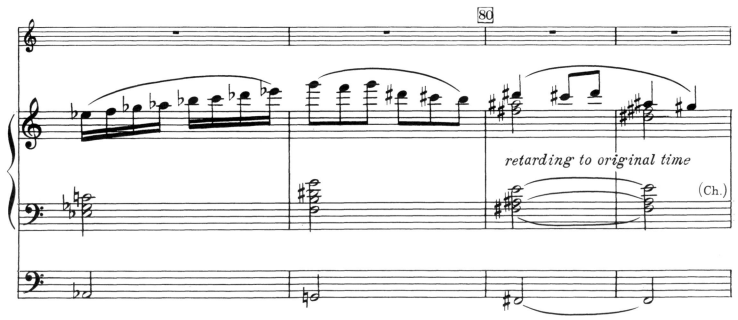

ritard slightly   **In time**

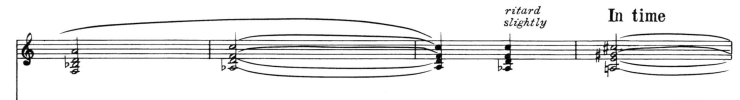

ISBN-13: 978-1-4950-1665-3

Distributed By

HAL LEONARD

50291630